Mind Control NOW:

A Powerful Guide to Manipulation, Persuasion and Human Psychology That Works!

Table Of Contents

Introduction

I want to thank you and congratulate you for downloading the book Mind Control NOW: A Powerful Guide to Manipulation, Persuasion and Human Psychology That Works!

This book contains proven steps and strategies on how to become a truly adept master of human psychology. This book contains tactics and guides on how to study human behavior and use that to your advantage. This book is made up of various techniques to be able to manipulate, persuade, or even deceive people. At the same time, learning these techniques would also allow you to avoid deception and make sure that you are able to prevent others from manipulating you into deluding yourself with a false notion.

Here's an inescapable fact: you will need to use any possible leverage that you have in order for you to expand your network and be able to open up opportunities to succeed. At the same time, you need to make sure that other people would be receptive to your ideas in any possible way. Now, a lot of people who are making a living out of selling their ideas are not aware that there are many ways to make sure that their words are being heard by their audience. At the same time, not a lot of people understand that through different language plays and careful observation of human behavior, they can create personal credibility. That knowledge alone creates unfair advantage in your favor!

If you do not develop your skills to observe human behavior and make manipulation, persuasion, and deception work to your advantage, you are not only missing out on a lot of opportunities; you are also practically letting others steal the available leverage from you by limiting your resources. This book is allowing you to see that every person that you meet is a customer that you can sell to. This book is making you aware that everyone in your network belongs to that group of people that you can influence.

It's time for you to become an amazing master of control, and this is the time for you to harness the power of human psychology and use it to your advantage. If you have felt that you are not being successful with pitching your ideas or selling any product, this book will turn the tables around for you. If you think that people around you have not been receptive of the things that you can do, this book will change that – you are going to be the master of your relationships and the dictator of your success.

The Fundamentals of Human Psychology and Manipulation, Persuasion, and Deception

The world is made up of two types of people: leaders and followers. People would always find that they are struggling to be at the top of the ladder, as if they are fighting to be at the top of the food chain. When you think about it, there must be a way in order for you to have the leverage to do so.

Understanding what moves the human mind would allow you to tap into this advantage. The fact that it is possible for most people to know what would allow people to buy your ideas already gives you the idea that you can even take the shortcut to the top. All you need to do is to find out what it is.

The Basis of Manipulation, Persuasion, and Deception

Having an unfair advantage over people is based on one single characteristic. When you observe people around you and understand what they are capable of making others think about them, you will notice that they all have the ability of being credible.

You need to keep this in mind: people are capable of deciding what is believable or not, and if you want to win them over to your line of thinking, they have to believe in you. They have to find that you have what it takes to lead them.

However, people will only follow other people that they can trust. You cannot expect strangers to just eradicate all their malicious thoughts about you when you try to sell them your idea. The reason is simple: people are taught at a very early age to not trust people that they do not know. They are taught that people who are outside the family all have the intention of getting the best of them. They are taught that nothing is free in this world – people who seem like they are doing them a favor would always ask for something in return.

You would come to think that you are raised by society this way as well. The doubt that people have in others serves as a shield to protect them from danger, and you know that there is no one on this planet who would ever put himself out there in order to follow a person that he does not know. For that reason, people believe in track records, testimonials, or anything else that will back up what they are being told to believe. People like evidence that ideas work. They do not believe that something can be too good to be true.

People believe in credibility because it puts order in their belief in society. It provides basis in the way that they think of others, because there is a premise in the way that they would view people who engage them. However, you will find that people have different ways of validating how people behave towards them. You will also see that there is a secret way of knowing what allows other people to believe that you can be a credible person to them.

The Ability to Transform Truth

After credibility comes a controller's ability to make target able to see their environment in a different way. While most of the time, controllers only want their targets to see things the way they see it, high-level controllers would want their targets to see that the decision they are pushing for is the most sensible choice to make in that situation.

Manipulation, persuasion, and deception aim to make the target feel that there is no other logical choice for them to make in a particular event. Controllers aim to minimize the credibility of their competitors, or to make other possible choices cease to exist. For that reason, controllers need to also manipulate how their targets would perceive truth, with the use of language alone.

You may ask if it is possible to even change what is true or not. For this reason, let's qualify what truth is. Truth is considered to be justified true belief, which means that a person needs to believe in something, and then find evidences that would support the claim. Since people behave differently and that they find the best support in different manners, you may see that people may uphold the same belief, but have different reasons for believing that.

You may not be able to change something for what it is. However, if you can present the evidences that would convince targets to see that your claim is true, then you are able to present to them your version of the truth. When you think about it, everyone else in the world is probably doing the same – they are all trying to present different scenarios to show people that their methods work. They may not be consciously doing it, but they know that they are trying to present their audience that there is only one correct approach to phenomena, or that what they are using is the best.

How is that "bending" the truth? Should one wish to stick to the rules of logic, you cannot ever classify something to be the best, unless you have tried every possible product out there. However, you know that you can't. You can't observe all the parts of the world at the same time and know what existing products there are that work the same way that yours do. That means that you are not able to make a real comparison with the others that would make you reach the conclusion that you have. But do you mean to lie? That is not the case most of the time. It is just the truth that you choose to justify for yourself.

All PR managers and advertisement companies operate on the same notion of belief. Products are being presented in the Internet, television, or radio the same way – they are being displayed as if they are the best choices to make, when in fact, they are the only choices that you see. Advertisements will never let you see any reason why you should not buy the product that they feature. Would you call that lying? You would probably not. After all, if you like the commercials that you see, you know that they are showing you the "truth" that you need to see in order for you to make a decision favorable to the manufacturer.

In essence, the ability of getting the better hand in human psychology is to always remember that being able to bend people's will to your favor would always involve two things – credibility and the presentation of truth. Now, find out how you can identify if you have what it takes to have control over people's minds.

Assuming the Role of the Controller

Being able to manipulate, deceive, or persuade means being able to become a psychological controller. When you reach the next chapters of this book, you would be able to get step-by-step guides on how to make sure that you are able to direct people to make choices that are favorable to you. However, before you spend time following those steps, it is important that you understand what it takes to be a controller, and how people really behave.

The Secret to Control

People will prefer to believe in you when you are someone that they like. And here is the secret to doing that: people tend to like themselves, and they would always feel attraction to people who are similar to them. That gives you the opportunity to create credibility.

That also means that people do not have to have evidence for your reliability, as long as you can make them see that you are likely to make the decisions that they make. All you need to do is to observe their behavior and mirror them.

What Makes Up Credibility

You will find that in some situations, you are not really certain that you are doing something 100% right. Sometimes, you are not even sure of what you are doing. However, there would always be that guy in the other cubicle who would always believe that if there is a person in the office who could do that specific task right, it would be you.

It might always the case that no matter what you do, you will always have the reputation of being a person who can make things happen. You may not appear that way to your boss or to some of your officemates, but it seems that this guy on the cubicle would do what it takes to push you towards your goal. You would also notice that it does not take too much effort for you to get him to do you a favor. He seems to be happy to help you succeed!

No, he does not think that you are perfect. He just likes you a lot as a person. That behavior towards you is a product of his previous experience with you, and he has a basis for believing what he sees in you.

Credibility is technically that positive impression that people have on others based on a particular stimulus. They see that it is possible for them to trust you despite the possibility that you will fail because of a particular precedent. If you have been reliable before, they are willing to give you the benefit of the doubt every time you show them your effort, and that they are likely to not think that you are trying to sell them an idea that they would never need in their life.

Credibility can also go another way – people are also likely to believe in your success if they see themselves in you, or that you are likely to have similar judgment. Why does that happen? People, no matter what their status is in life, are bound to not second guess themselves. They would always want to believe that they are making the right decisions, and if they see that you are likely to behave the same way that they do, they are likely to believe in the idea that you are trying to make them accept.

In other words, you can create credibility if you are able to either make another person experience that you are reliable, or make them see that the actions that you choose to make would be similar to their choices. Now, you would notice that the way that you can create a favorable reputation to yourself involves two periods of occurrence – the past and the future. Which is the much easier route?

Looking at how you can possibly create a positive reputation, you know that you can only control what will happen today, which will eventually change the future. You know that you cannot go back and change their experience of you. However, you can change the way that they will perceive you from now on.

Understanding Other People

While this book will tell you how to manipulate, persuade, or deceive others, this is not a book of black magic that would instantly make people's nature about these practices disappear. However, this book will teach you how to operate based on people's preferences and make them convince themselves that they are right to see, feel, and hear things your way.

The key to being successful in "bending" people's minds is to understand that people would not choose to be forcefully changed. Everybody have a concept of how they can grasp the world, and they are very comfortable with the way they handle their behavior towards others. If you suddenly appear in their lives and begin ordering them what to do, you are likely to face walls that you cannot break down even when you try doing so for decades.

If you want to be able to change people, you have to understand that they also want to do the same to you. They would want to believe that you are experiencing the same world, and for that reason, you are also able to see that they are able to make the right decisions for themselves. At the same time, they would also see that you are likely to make the right suggestions that they should listen to, because you are also able to walk the same shoes that they are in.

It does not pay to tell people that they have been doing what they are doing the wrong way, unless you have figured it out by going through a similar process. If you have been born rich, you cannot tell a homeless man that he has a wrong approach when it comes to making a living. You cannot tell another person what to do, if you haven't ever experienced doing it the same way they would in their situation.

That is why persuasion, manipulation, and deception techniques come in handy. No matter how try to walk into somebody else's shoes, you cannot duplicate the way they experience the world around them. Their ideas about their society are unique and you cannot possibly guess what their next decision could be. However, understanding how people perceive their world allows you to make intelligent guesses. Through hypotheses, you can identify a list of palatable choices that you can offer them.

Different People and the Way They Choose

When you try to understand human behavior, you would realize that people make decisions according to their experiences. The way that they react to the world and the knowledge that they embrace all depends on the way they were taught to make decisions. That means that people's knowledge of the world is mostly governed by forces that they do not really control. As long as people are part of societies, their decisions would be mostly molded by the environments that they are in.

People may think that they are free to decide, but when you choose to study human history, you will discover that that is not the case. They are making decisions that are based on comfort and avoidance of pain. As long as they see a particular choice to provide them more benefits than disadvantages, they are more likely to jump into that decision without thinking twice. These decisions are mostly influenced by their experience within the society, and the past decisions that they have made that either provided them pleasure or pain.

In order for you to better understand people's decision-making behavior, here's a classification of individuals that you may encounter, based on how they create personal choices.

The People of the Bandwagon

There are people who make decisions based on how society conditioned them, as if decisions are merely indoctrinated in them. Most of their decisions are based on large social or personal relationships, and they are the ones that are mostly influenced by generalizations and bandwagons. You will also notice that they normally think that they have situations that do not exist, and they always fall to their irrational fear. They are also egocentric, and as long as they think that a particular product is targeted towards people like them, they buy it immediately.

These people are the ones who like short-term pleasures, and they often judge people according to stereotype. They are also the ones who have definite conviction of the good and evil. They also believe that there is a simple and singular approach to life.

These are the people that are often the target of mass media and propaganda. Most of the commercials that you see on TV are also made to cater to such audience. Most of the time, these people are the ones that are most knowledgeable about the local news and the latest trends.

Self-Interested Decision Makers

Within every social circle is a small group of people who believe that they are the kings and queens of their society. They may not wield political power, but they believe that they need to pursue their own interests without regard for the benefit of the majority or how people around them would feel. They prefer to exude themselves as sophisticated or the better-learned and they are the ones that are well-versed with rhetoric. Because of their unrelenting effort to be always at the top, they are often found in the higher throes of society.

While they believe that they are better off than the rest of society, they do not act as rebels or critical minded. In fact, they prefer to associate themselves with people with high authority, such as politicians or national superstars.

Understanding the behavior of these two groups of people would make you aware that there are people who decide according to what would give them leverage over people, or they would want to be of the same status as others. You would see that people have different motivations when it comes to their decisions, based on how they operate within the society. You now know how to approach these two types of people, and you also know what would probably allow them to agree to establish a relationship with you.

Understanding the Buyer's Behavior

You will observe that people would always find reasons why they prefer the things that they like. Once that they have already acquired or bought a property, they would be able to tell all the reasons that they have in mind on why they find such an item beneficial to them. Even if they are not even using it at the moment, they can imagine how such item can help them in the future!

However, you would notice that people always work with this behavior in a linear fashion – they realize how badly they wanted that item right after they have acquired it. You would also notice that there are people who seem to know the feeling of having an item already, even if they have merely seen it on television or on a Facebook page. There is something that advertisements do to people to make them crave for the products being advertised whether they really need these things or not.

Advertisements and promo managers understand buyers' behavior. How people come to crave for things that they have not experienced yet can be easily triggered. You will find that people can be convinced to buy items when they are told that they will provide the same feeling they had when they purchased the last thing they bought.

The same rule may be applied when you are selling yourself. You would also notice how certain people tend to like actors or movie characters so much that they even feel that they are so smart or lovable even if they have not even met them before. However, they realize that those characters, real or not, have something in common with them. Knowing this allows you to take advantage – all you need to do is to provide your target the idea that you are similar to them.

Can You Sell Yourself Immediately?

Is it possible for people to build instant connections? Yes it is, but it comes with preparation. Unless it is very coincidental that you are very similar to your target (e.g. you tend to shop for similar clothes, have the same mannerisms, or that you tend to have identical beliefs), then you can. However, it happens rarely.

What can you do to make sure that you can establish a relationship quickly? You have to first observe how a person behaves and find out what you have in common. It might be an interest or a certain religious belief. You may also try to find out if your parents went to the same school or if you took the same course in college. Once you are able to find out your common denominator, you will feel that you are comfortable enough to move towards build rapport.

However, you will feel that sometimes, whenever you make a sudden move to build a relationship, your target starts to meet your effort with resistance. They seem to find you dubious and that there is malice in your intentions. They begin to think that you want something from them but they can never expect anything in return. They feel that your only goal is to manipulate them into doing something for you.

Rapport is built successfully if the target does not sense that you are only trying to build a relationship for a personal gain. While it is obvious that people may want to make relationships to use it for their advantage, targets want to always feel that they have control over their intentions. That goes the same even if you are trying to assume the role of the controller. You would need to make the other person aware that you are willing to enter a compromise and provide a deal that would be for mutual benefit. However, you have to understand that even if you have such intentions from the start, people do not recognize it immediately. For that reason, you should learn how to pace with your target before moving to sell yourself.

The next chapter will tell you about the most effective way of building rapport and how you can move from building a relationship into persuading, manipulating, or deceiving your target.

The Golden Tactics for Manipulation

Psychological manipulation is the practice of bending one's will by determining the vulnerabilities of a target when it comes to making decisions. What makes it possible to manipulate other people is one's ability to bend one's conviction of the truth.

Some psychologists believe that manipulation is coercive, that a manipulator should force a certain belief upon another person through any possible aggressive means. Looking back at the definition of the word, it holds a certain truth – after all, manipulation means exhausting the weak points that you can spot in a person's ability to create his personal beliefs.

Manipulation is commonly built upon these foundations:

1. Ability to make use of logical fallacies

2. Concealment of aggressive behavior

3. Belief reinforcement

Why do these elements go well together? While information can be logically fallible and that it is definitely absurd to believe, a manipulator enforces that incredible belief upon his target to attack a specific belief. For a target to not suspect it, the manipulator reinforces the "correctness" of the decision that he wants the target to do instead. When a person refuses to change his earlier belief to favor the manipulator, the latter would subtly use aggression, such as the enforcement of fear, to change the target's mind. The process goes on and on, until the manipulator manages to get the decision that is favorable for him.

How to Manipulate

When you are moving to manipulate your target, the best way to do it subtly is to present your idea as the only way to prevent pain or the only way to promote pleasure. With that said, that means that your target will see that there is no other choice but to make that decision.

How would your target come across the idea that the option that you are offering him is the best choice to make? You will observe that people are most likely to react and make decisions quickly when they are under duress. If they feel that their comfort is being attacked, they would be quick to choose the option that they believe would make them feel safe again.

Here are some of the time-tested manipulation tactics that you should keep in mind:

Appealing to Fear

One of the most effective approaches of manipulation is appealing to fear, which is probably the most common fallacy that you can use. When people fear that they are going to place themselves or their loved ones in danger, they feel that they are backed into a corner and they do not have any other choice but to accept the deal that the controller offers.

You would see that this is also one of the best-known techniques in advertisements, especially those that promote sanitary products such as cleaning detergents and bug sprays. Television tries to display that if you do not buy these products, your family will get sick or that your house would be overrun by roaches and mosquitoes. While that is not likely to be true, you buy those products anyway because of the image that they bring to your mind.

Turning Tables

Another skill of manipulators is to turn the scenario around by making the other person appear guilty of the very thing that they are being accused of. For example, a controller may divert accusations against him by making the accuser appear guilty of the similar thing. That would distract the accuser and put the other person on the defensive.

Appealing to Pity

People are emotional creatures – they tend to be manipulated when they feel that someone else is under a far worse situation than they are. It is the same appeal that your parents would have given you when you do not want to eat your vegetables – for some reason, they bring up the starvation issue in impoverished countries in order for you to eat the food that the people in those countries cannot have.

Pity is a powerful emotion that can cripple critical thinking – it allows people to see that they are in a better off state than the manipulator, and that is being perpetuated by the "opportunity" that the manipulator proposes. Since people want to feel good about themselves, manipulators take advantage of the fact that they can make targets feel good about themselves when they take the option that they want them to have.

The Golden Tactics for Persuasion

When you are trying to build credibility, the first thing that you need to keep in mind is that it is not enough to make the other person open up to you. Apart from making your target like you enough to engage you, you need to create a special relationship with him, before aiming to introduce him to your agenda. When aiming to persuade someone, the controller needs to understand how to build a good relationship with his target to win him over and adopt his point of view.

This chapter also holds the secret to being able to sell any type of service or product, and make sure that you would be able to get better leads, depending on how your relationship with the target progresses. At the same time, this chapter would enable you to identify buying behavior, and address them appropriately.

Pacing

Pacing, otherwise called mirroring, is the subtle imitation of the target's behavior. This trick allows the target to feel that the controller is similar to him, which allows you to break down barriers whenever you are going in for the kill.

Pacing is tricky because it really is an issue of timing. If the target feels you are trying to search for the common ground and he feels that there is insincerity in your similarity, he is likely to build resistance. If you move to slow, the opportunity to build a relationship and take control is lost. The best way to pace is to maintain synchronicity until he notices that you are naturally similar. When that happens, you can proceed to the next step, which is leading.

Leading

This part is where you move towards the goal while you are pacing with the target. You would notice that you are able to mentally do that, without any verbal cue to the target, when you try to pace his walking for a few minutes, and then suddenly change the way you swing your hands or the speed of your walking. Your target would subconsciously follow your behavior, even if you do not give him any verbal command.

When you are trying to sell anything to a target, it is very important for you to know the best opportunity to maneuver his behavior. You would learn soon that the best time to do it is when you feel that there is enough trust between you and your target, and that you can make him enter a situation wherein he can believe that you have something in your hands that would address his needs. The good thing is that most people discuss their needs with the person that they trust, as long as they can think that they are likely to make mutual decisions, or that they tend to react towards certain stimulus the same way. When that happens, you are ready to move closer towards your goal.

What Rapport Really Is

Rapport is not just a relationship based on your target's attraction to you, but more importantly, it should be a relationship that is built on trust. You may think that you just need to make the other person trust you, but in reality, it is not – you also need to be confident that at the end of your engagement, you will come up with a positive agreement with the other person.

There are times that you think that you will be able to walk away with a good sale, or that you will be able to make your target sign a deal with you. You may have a good time together, but it seems like your target is still gunning to make your traditional roles stick to just the way it is – you as the salesman and him the savvy buyer. What happened there?

From that example, it seems that you are not able to meet the main goal of the relationship that you built, which is mutual trust. However, there are ways to be able to secure a good relationship from the start, and then make sure that you are able to detect instances when the rapport you are establishing is falling apart.

In order for you to get a good relationship with a person that you are trying to sell your idea or a product to, these are the steps that you need to follow. Note that these steps are not necessarily followed in a linear fashion – you will find that there are situations wherein you need to go back to a previous step in order to progress.

1. Make Your Target Invite You to Sell

Securing the invitation to offer anything is possibly one of the most crucial steps that you need to make when you are trying to influence a person. Without this invitation, your target is not likely to listen to anything that you have to say. Forcing yourself to sell would only make your target resist you, which would damage any future chance of getting him to make the decision that you prefer.

It would be easy to secure the invitation in person, because the other person gets the immediate impression that you can be like him. You can also pay attention to his behavior, which gives you the ability to pace him. Once he recognizes that you are trying to approach him based on your common ground, you are most likely to get an invitation.

Securing an invitation over the phone is more difficult – you would need to make sure that you can pace with his tone and have a rather accurate hypothesis of his physical behavior. Keep in mind that you also have shorter time to get your target's attention over the phone. Make sure that you get it within 10 seconds, or else the opportunity to sell is lost.

2. Establish Rapport

Once you are able to make sure that your target has sent you the signal to continue, move to establish your relationship immediately. Do not attempt to sell your target anything yet – make sure that your target trusts you enough to tell you what he really needs.

Once you find out your target's preference, make sure that you connect the idea that you are offering to his needs. That will make him more receptive to your proposal.

3. Get into an Agreement

This is the part wherein you get the other person to commit to your proposal by making him agree to compromise so you can enter a win-win agreement. Sell your idea through consultation, by asking him what the best situations are that you can offer in order for him to enter into an agreement with you. This is the part wherein the target would most likely raise questions regarding your idea. When this happens, there are probably parts of your proposal that are not explained adequately. Do not immediately jump into the conclusion that your target is about to withdraw from the rapport – it might be the opportunity for you to bring out additional features, or to clarify benefits.

Note that this is the part wherein the other person may feel that he is not prepared to do the decision that you are leading him to, and he may revert into a more dismissive role – you may soon find him telling you that there is nothing that he can do about the situation, or that he is simply shopping around.

When that happens, find out where the resistance is coming from. You might have failed to recognize his other needs, and it seems like you are not able to offer him the entire package that he wants. Secure the invitation to continue, or maybe get another appointment instead. If you have been doing rapport correctly, you will find that the other person is not willing to drop your connection – he would still be willing to do other favors for you.

4. Go for the Close

If you were able to do all the other steps right, getting the other person to do what you want him to do should not be difficult. However, if you feel that you are unable to build adequate rapport or you did not have enough opportunity to lead him to the choice that you prefer, be prepared to realign your goals.

Any skilled psychological controller would know how to redefine his goals, depending on how steps 2 and 3 went. If he feels that the target seems hesitant, it might be a good closing move to talk to the person some other time instead, and redefine the ways he could establish rapport. That makes the other person feel that he is valuable, and that he should give more interest to the idea being offered. That is a safe move if you are confident that you were able to provide all the benefits and features that he needs to know about your idea. That is also a good move if you are sure that the target likes you.

If you think that you cannot convert this person into a buyer, ask for someone else that you can close. That makes the other person refer your idea to someone else, which he thinks you can close easily. When that happens, the rapport that you have made with the target will still be put to good use.

The Golden Tactics for Deception

Deception is probably one of the most self-explanatory concepts in this book – it is the practice of omitting the truth from the target, to either sway his opinion to something favorable for the controller, or to avoid a difficult situation.

Every controller needs to have deceptive skills, because these would be valuable when one needs to be on the defensive. It is also one of the best ways to extract information from another person, especially when that target is very unwilling to divulge his knowledge. When manipulation does not appear to work, deception becomes the most viable option for a controller.

Here are some of the deceptive tactics that one can use for defensive stances, swaying one's opinion, or extracting information.

Misdirection

This tactic, often popular with magicians, is the practice of making the target pay attention to specific event, while the controller does a trick in another setting. This is one of the tricks that one can do in order to deceive the target in order to conceal a particular truth. This is being done in order for the controller to make the target believe a specific notion. The concealment is very effective because it hides the option that the controller does not want the target to see – that way, the controller makes the target make the option that he prefers.

Understatement

This is a tactic that can be used to make the target feel that the part of the truth is irrelevant. With this trick, the controller makes the target dismiss the choice that he does not want, which minimizes the risk of any event turning out to be unfavorable.

Downplaying parts of the truth is a very effective way to defend one's self from being exposed, or it makes a particular accuser's allegations irrelevant. It is very similar to burying the evidence, or hiding the ugly parts of a product for sale. With the concealment, the target believes that he is looking at a very favorable option that is very logical to choose. He does not know, however, that there would be a catch afterwards.

Exaggeration

The exact opposite of understatement, this tactic is aimed to make the target not notice the entire truth, but only see the portion of it that would be enough for him to make a decision favorable to the controller. In order for the target to feel that he has seen compelling evidence that he is making the right choice, the controller aims to make a fragment of the truth seem to be such a big deal. Ultimately, the controller distracts the target with the rewarding part of the choice, by making it look like it is the entire picture.

Outright Lying

While omission or bending of certain parts of the truth to make them appear larger is already considered lying, an outright lie is the deliberate manipulation of truth by stating that a knowledge that is contrary to what is present. It happens when the controller says a statement that is very different or the opposite from the truth.

Some Notes on How Deception Works

In order for deception to work, the controller must always operate in such a way that it is impossible for the target to detect or suspect manipulation of the truth. At the same time, controllers must always make sure that that should in any case the target suspects that there is something amiss, the controller would need to make sure that he can redirect the attention of the target into something to make a strategic exit.

The bad thing about deception is that once the target is able to think that the controller is hiding something, it is virtually impossible for him to redeem his position – the target is most likely to think that the controller is not likely to tell the truth. Keep in mind that targets who sensed that they are being deceived are very likely to not participate with the controller.

Should it happen, the best way to gain the confidence and establish credibility is to ensure that you build rapport with the target and then engage him using a different tactic. You may try to use persuasion instead so you can be able to identify his needs and talk to him into making a deal that would allow you to discuss ways for both of you to enjoy mutual benefit. Make sure that you consult with the target in order for you to identify areas in his behavior that would make susceptible to your tactics – that would allow you to break down the wall that he has built to defend himself from you. Afterwards, you would be able to make sure that he is willing to open himself to your ideas.

Conclusion

Thank you again for downloading this book!

I hope this book was able to help you to learn more about human behavior and how people can be swayed to make decisions that are beneficial to you.

The next step is to discover ways to use the techniques that are discussed in this book.

Finally, if you enjoyed this book, please take the time to share your thoughts and post a review on Amazon. It'd be greatly appreciated!

Thank you and good luck!

www.ingramcontent.com/pod-product-compliance
Lightning Source LLC
Chambersburg PA
CBHW070257290526
45789CB00004B/1879